HERE'S THE SCOOP

FOLLOW AN ICE-CREAM CONE AROUND THE WORLD

Neale S. Godfrey

The One-and-Only Common Sense Series ™
(cents)

Illustrated by
Randy Verougstraete

Modern Curriculum Press
Parsippany, New Jersey

M000105675

To my nieces and nephews—Dana, Jason, Max, Trevor, and Whitney.
I'm really proud to be your Aunt Neale.

To Mom—You're such a great friend.
To King Sock and Bug Man—I couldn't have asked for two finer brothers.
Randy Verougstraete

Modern Curriculum Press
An imprint of Pearson Learning
299 Jefferson Road, P.O. Box 480
Parsippany, New Jersey 07054-0480
www.pearsonlearning.com
1-800-321-3106

1 2 3 4 5 6 7 8 9 10 SP 05 04 03 02 01 00

ISBN 0-7652-1761-9

Modern
Curriculum
Press

There is excitement in the town of Green$treet$.
A crowd is standing in front of Bull and Bear's store, the Blue Chip Deli.
Everyone is trying to read the big sign in the window.

FREE ICE CREAM

The Green$treet$ Kids—

Penny Bright,

Dollar Bill, better known as Buck,

Hedge,

Small Change,

Short Cut, and

Ona Budget

wait in line to get inside the store.

Bull and Bear are standing behind the counter.
They are giving out tiny blue spoons and
teeny-weeny cups of ice cream.

"I'd like to invent my own new flavor," said Buck.

"Sure, I bet it's easy to make ice cream," added Hedge.

"Easy? You must be kidding!
It's not easy to make ice cream!" said Penny.
"It takes cows and trees
        and beans and plants
                and trucks and . . . ."

"You don't find those things in ice cream," said Penny.
"You need them to make ice cream.
If you don't believe me . . .
just ask Mr. Possibility."

"He always finds a way
to figure things out!"
added Small Change.

·BILLBOARD·
In 1846, Nancy Johnson invented
the first ice-cream maker.
It had a hand crank that
mixed everything up.

8

The GreenStreets Kids hurried to Mr. Possibility's workshop. When they got there, Mr. Possibility was busy working on his Zowie-Wowie World Whizzer!

9

"Oh, I just love ice cream," said Mr. Possibility.
"This is a great chance to test out my Zowie-Wowie World Whizzer!
Hop in, kids.
Fasten your seatbelts.

We're going to follow
an ice-cream cone
around the world!"

11

"Wow!" exclaimed Buck.

"Where are we?" asked Small Change.

"We're flying over a dairy farm in Wisconsin," explained Mr. Possibility. "The farmer milks the cows and sells the milk."

"Those big trucks are delivering the milk to an ice-cream factory," said Penny.

"You need milk to make ice cream," said Hedge.

"So that's why you need cows!" exclaimed Buck.

"And trucks!" added Ona.

"You're getting it!" replied Mr. Possibility.

13

"It's time to move on," said Mr. Possibility.
"Now, let's go to Costa Rica to find out about sugar."

14

"That grass sure is tall!" exclaimed Short Cut.

"That's not grass, it's sugar cane," said Penny.

"Sugar comes from sugar cane," said Mr. Possibility.
"It takes a lot of people and a lot of work to make sugar."

Wow!

15

"First the sugar cane is grown," explained Mr. Possibility.
"Then it's cut."

·BILLBOARD·
Sugar cane can grow as tall
as a two-story house.

16

"After that, the sugar cane is
crushed,
cooked,
bleached,
and dried.
At last, it looks like the sugar we eat!"

"Finally the sugar is sent by trucks,
   ships, and trains
      to places around the world," Mr. Possibility added.

"Places like ice-cream factories," said Penny.

SUGAR

"So far, we know there's milk and sugar in ice cream," said Hedge.

"What other stuff is in ice cream?" asked Buck.

"Let's find out!" exclaimed Ona.

"Look, we've landed in Madagascar!" exclaimed Penny.
"Vanilla beans are grown here."

"Does vanilla come from vanilla beans?" asked Small Change.

"Let's get out and take a look," said Mr. Possibility.

· BILLBOARD ·
Madagascar is a country off
the eastern coast of Africa.
A lot of vanilla beans are grown there.

20

Mr. Possibility explained, "Vanilla beans come from flowers called orchids.
The vanilla beans are picked and then sent to a factory.
In the factory the beans are made into a vanilla liquid.
This liquid is what is added to ice cream to give it a vanilla flavor."

"First, milk, then sugar, then vanilla—I guess that must be everything we need for vanilla ice cream!" exclaimed Buck.

" But my favorite flavor is mint chocolate chip," said Penny. "What goes into that flavor?"

"Oh wowie, zowie," said Mr. Possibility. "Let's take off and I'll show you!"

23

"Right now we're flying over fields of mint plants in Australia," said Mr. Possibility.

"But where are the chocolate chips?" asked Short Cut.

24

"Take a look down there," said Mr. Possibility.
"Those are cacao trees in Brazil.
Chocolate comes from cacao beans."

"Cacao beans are dried,
    roasted, crushed, and
        sent by trucks, ships, and
            trains to places around the world," said Penny.

"And now I want an ice-cream cone!" said Mr. Possibility.
"How about you?
Next stop is the ice-cream factory!"

·BILLBOARD·
The ice-cream cone was introduced by accident
at the 1904 World's Fair in St. Louis.
An ice-cream seller ran out of dishes,
so the waffle-maker molded his waffles into cones.

"Who pays for everything that goes into ice cream?" asked Short Cut.

"You do!" said Penny.

"The money you spend for an ice-cream cone pays for the milk, the sugar, the vanilla, and everything else in the ice cream," explained Mr. Possibility.

"How do people find out about new flavors of ice cream?" asked Hedge.

"Well, we had a free taste of bubble-gum sneaker ice cream at the Blue Chip Deli," said Ona.

"Can you think of other ways to find out about something new?" asked Mr. Possibility.

30

"We could try to make our own ice cream," suggested Penny.

"First we need a recipe," said Ona.

"But we don't have to fly around the world," added Hedge.
"We can just go to the supermarket for the ingredients."

"Count me in.
I've got plenty of change!" said Small Change.

PENNY BRIGHT'S
MINT CHOCOLATE CHIP ICE CREAM

(This activity should take place under adult supervision.)

INGREDIENTS

1 teaspoon unflavored gelatin

1 tablespoon cold water

2 tablespoons hot water

$\frac{1}{2}$ cup whole milk

$\frac{1}{3}$ cup sugar

2 teaspoons vanilla extract

$\frac{1}{4}$ teaspoon peppermint extract

1 cup heavy cream

1 milk chocolate candy bar

Place the mixing bowl and beaters in the freezer
one hour before you begin making ice cream.

Put the unflavored gelatin in a medium-sized bowl.
Add the cold water. Let the gelatin soften.

Have an adult add the hot water.
Stir until the gelatin dissolves.

Add milk, sugar, vanilla extract, and peppermint extract.
Mix until the sugar dissolves.

Take the mixing bowl and beaters out of the freezer.
Pour the heavy cream into the cold bowl and beat until stiff.

Gently mix the milk-and-sugar mixture into the whipped cream.
Pour the mixture into a metal ice-cube tray
(without the ice-cube separators) or loaf pan.
Cover it with plastic wrap and place in the freezer.

When the mixture starts to freeze, take it out of the freezer.
Pour the mixture back into the mixing bowl and beat again.
Return the mixture to the ice-cube tray or loaf pan and freeze.

Once the ice cream starts to freeze again, take it out of the
freezer a second time and beat it.

Break the chocolate bar into small pieces.
Mix the chocolate pieces into the ice cream and freeze again.
When the ice cream is completely frozen, take it out and eat it!